Really WILD

BEARS

Claire Robinson

Heinemann
LIBRARY

First published in Great Britain by Heinemann Library
Halley Court, Jordan Hill, Oxford OX2 8EJ,
a division of Reed Educational and Professional Publishing Ltd.

OXFORD FLORENCE PRAGUE MADRID ATHENS
MELBOURNE AUCKLAND KUALA LUMPUR SINGAPORE TOKYO
IBADAN NAIROBI KAMPALA JOHANNESBURG GABORONE
PORTSMOUTH NH (USA) CHICAGO MEXICO CITY SAO PAULO

Designed by Celia Floyd
Illustrations by Alan Fraser (Pennant Illustration) and Hardlines (map p.6)
Colour reproduction by Dot Gradations.
Printed in Hong Kong / China

01 00 99 98
10 9 8 7 6 5 4 3 2 1

ISBN 0 431 02863 X

British Library Cataloguing in Publication Data

Robinson, Claire
Bears. – (Really wild)
1. Bears – Juvenile literature
I. Title
599.6'1

This book is also available as a hardback library edition (ISBN 0 431 02862 1)

Flick the pages of this book and see what happens!

Acknowledgements
The Publishers would like to thank the following for permission to reproduce photographs:
Oxford Scientific Films: Matthias Breiter, p.7; Daniel J Cox, pp.9, 16; David C Fritts, pp.15, 20; Djuro Huber, p.17; Frank Huber, pp.4 (left), 12; G C Kelley, p.21; Jeff Lepore, p.13; Zig Leszczynski, p.4 (right); C.C. Lockwood, p.8; James McCann, p.11; Joe McDonald, p.5 (left); Tom Mettugh, p.10; Meyers, p.6; Norbert Rosing, p.5 (right); Leonard Lee Rue, p.18; Frank Schneidermeyer, p.22; Stouffer Productions, p.19; Ronald Toms, p.23; Jim Zipp, p.14.
Cover photograph: Bruce Coleman Ltd/John Shaw

Our thanks to Oxford Scientific Films for their help and co-operation in the preparation of this book.

Every effort has been made to contact copyright holders of any material reproduced in this book. Any omissions will be rectified in subsequent printings if notice is given to the Publisher.

Contents

Some words are shown in bold, **like this**. You can find out what they mean by looking in the glossary.

Bear relatives

Bears are some of the world's biggest **mammals**. There are seven different kinds of bear. Here you can see some of them.

brown bear

sloth bear

sun bear

polar bear

Polar bears are the largest bears. Sun bears are the smallest. This book is about brown bears.

Where brown bears live

Brown bears live in forests and mountains in Canada, Alaska and Russia. A few live in Europe. In Canada and Alaska, they are called **grizzly** bears.

Some brown bears live on the cold **Arctic tundra**. There are no trees there and food is hard to find. The bears in this book live in Alaska.

Males and females

Brown bears like to live on their own.
This big male stands up to see if there are
any other bears nearby. He will scare
them away. Look at his sharp claws.

Female bears live on their own, except when they have **cubs**. This female will look after her cubs for two to four years.

Mating

In the early summer, the male bear travels a long way to find a **mate**. If he meets another male bear, they will fight. Male bears are very fierce.

At last, the male finds a female. He stays
with her for a week or two. After they
have **mated**, he will leave her.

Finding food

The bears spend many hours looking for food. They eat a lot of grass and berries. They dig the ground with their sharp claws to find insects and small **mammals**.

Bears have a very good sense of smell and a good memory. This **cub** sniffs some tasty food. She will remember this feeding place. She may come back to it.

Fishing

Brown bears in Canada and Alaska are huge and eat a lot of fish. This **grizzly** is trying to catch a **salmon**. He leans forward hungrily.

14

Many other bears have arrived. There is
plenty of food for everyone. The bears are
so busy fishing, there is no time to fight.

Winter is coming

It is autumn. Soon snow will cover the plants and there will be no insects. The bears eat as much as they can and grow fat. They will eat nothing all winter.

During the long winter months, the bears sleep in **dens**. They make a hole under rocks or trees. This female will sleep in her den for about six months.

Babies

The **cubs** are born in the winter. Here, they are ten days old. Their eyes are still closed. They drink their mother's milk and keep warm in her fur.

In spring, the mother and her cubs leave
the **den**. The snow begins to melt. This
cub is three months old and he loves to play.

Growing up

The **cubs** learn fast. They watch their
mother catch a fish. They already know
how to sniff the ground to find insects
and roots.

This young bear is now two. He still travels with his mother and sister. He learns to watch for danger. In about a year's time, he will go to live on his own.

Brown bear facts

- Bears mainly eat plants. They also catch small **mammals** such as ground squirrels and rabbits. Sometimes they hunt young deer, too.

- Bears usually give birth to two to four **cubs** at a time, but two cubs is the most common.

- Brown bears can live for 25 years.

- Bears rub their backs against trees to leave their smell. This warns other bears that they are nearby.

- Brown bears used to live in Britain over 900 years ago.

- A bear's claws are 10 cm long. That's probably longer than twice the length of your longest finger!

Glossary

Arctic   the cold, northern part of the world

cub   a baby bear

den   a safe, warm hole in the ground

grizzly   what brown bears are called in Canada
            and Alaska

mammal   an animal with hair that feeds its babies
            on milk

mate   a partner to have babies with

mating   two animals making a baby together

salmon   a type of large fish

tundra   land in the Arctic that is covered by low
            growing plants, and where the soil is frozen
            most of the year

Index